D1369491

Knowing the Father

A Six-Week Bible Study
To Understand God's
Father-Like Attributes

Lisa Burkhardt Worley

Knowing the Father
A Six-Week Bible Study
By Lisa Burkhardt Worley

www.PearlsOfPromiseMinistries.com

Published by:
Pearls of Promise Ministries

Dedication

To my husband, Jeff, for supporting this
calling of God on my life.

And to all who desire a more intimate
relationship with their Heavenly Father.

Acknowledgements

Thanks to my friend Frank Ball for sharing his giftedness by creating the book cover and formatting this study.

Thanks to Katie Smith for doing an excellent job of editing *Knowing the Father*.

Thanks to our Pearls of Promise Team: Rosemary Legrand, Dr. Lynnette Simm, Aurora Ortega Geis, and Alma Jimenez Hall for your encouragement, hard work, and loyalty to this ministry.

Introduction

My dad was a physician who died suddenly while competing in a polo match, two months before I was born. Because I never knew my father, for many years I saw God as a distant being who reigned from his lofty throne—someone who did not need, nor desire, a relationship with me. I was afraid of God because he represented the unknown, was far greater than my mind could comprehend, and seemed unreachable in my humanness.

What I've found is that I'm not alone in this concept of God. For most fatherless people, it's not natural to have a close, intimate relationship with God if our earthly father was not active in our lives. However, if our father was absent because of death or abandonment, physically or emotionally, we cannot transfer the attributes of a human father to that of a holy and loving God. Instead, we have to be open to the possibility that God is far different from our earthly fathers. We must examine what the Bible says about him and believe the truth stated in 1 John 3:1: "See what great love the Father has lavished on us, that we should be called children of God! And that is what we are!"

After writing my book, *The Only Father I Ever Knew,* I realized there needed to be a companion Bible study focusing on the attributes of our heavenly Father, so that through God's Word, readers could grasp the Father heart of our Creator. While there are countless attributes of God as a perfect Father, I asked Abba Daddy to show me the six attributes he wanted his children to understand most, and he was faithful to provide.

As you delve into this study, I pray you draw closer to God the Father and develop a love for him like never before. He desires a vibrant, intimate relationship with you and wants you to know how much he cares for you, dear child of God!

Lisa Burkhardt Worley

Table of Contents

Week One: Pursuer

There were five minutes left in English class, and our teacher had completed her lesson. I was a freshman in high school, already headed down the wrong road because of no direction at home due to my fatherlessness and a mother who struggled emotionally. I was noticing boys and experimenting with drinking so I'd feel more comfortable around other people. However, in that five-minute window, my life changed forever. The friend sitting in front of me, Leslie, wasted no time by turning around and asking me if I wanted to accept Jesus as my Lord and Savior. I didn't know much about God or Jesus, because we were not regular churchgoers, but the concept seemed intriguing, and I prayed, not knowing where this would lead, to receive Jesus as the Lord and Savior of my life.

When I look back on that day, I realize that God pursued me through my friend. He placed her in front of me in class, and he gave her the idea and the boldness to ask the question. At that moment he stepped into my life to invite me into his family.

God has a heart for those who are fatherless and desires to be the father they never had. Psalm 68:5 says, "A father to the fatherless, a defender of widows, is God in his holy dwelling."

Have you ever thought about how God pursued you? Perhaps He's pursuing you right now through this study. So this week, let's discover how God pursues us to draw us into a relationship with him.

Day One

**Our Father pursues us through an audible voice
or impression upon our spirit.**

One of the best examples of this is found in the book of 1 Samuel, Chapter 1, where Samuel's mother, Hannah, was barren and desired a child. So one day, she traveled to the Jewish tabernacle in Shiloh and in deep anguish, prayed that God would open her womb. She promised that if her prayer for a baby was answered, then she would give him back to the Lord for all the days of his life. God was gracious to Hannah as she became pregnant with Samuel. Out of her gratitude, as promised, she presented her son back to God for service with the high priest, Eli. Samuel would eventually become the prophet and ruler over Israel, but God introduced himself to Samuel first, making himself real to him when he was only a child. Through your study today, find out how God pursued Samuel.

1. Read 1 Samuel 3:1–21.

2. How did God pursue Samuel?

3. How did he finally understand the voice was from God?

4. What did God tell him?

5. What was Samuel's relationship with his heavenly Father like after this encounter?

6. How has Father God pursued you? How does he continue to pursue you?

7. Samuel was pursued for a purpose. What purpose has God revealed for your life?

Day Two

Our Father pursues us through other people.

For about five years, I was in charge of public relations at an airport. When there were openings on my staff, I used to pray that God would bring women I could mentor and perhaps lead to Christ. I am pleased to say that two women know God as Father today because he used me as a conduit to reach them. Who in your world desperately needs to know God and his salvation through Jesus Christ? Living a good life before others is not enough. Romans 10:17 says, "Consequently, faith comes from hearing the message, and the message is heard through the word about Christ." We must speak the word of truth to others. He uses us to reach his people through verbal outreach. In today's study, we'll look at how God pursued the first recorded convert in Europe, Lydia, through the obedience of the Apostle Paul.

1. Read Acts 16:1–15.

2. Where did Paul travel to?

3. What was his initial plan and how did that change?

4. Who was Lydia and how did she respond?

5. Were you pursued by God through another person? How did you respond?

6. Why is it important to always be ready to shift gears and share the Gospel like Paul did? Read 1 Peter 3:15 and Matthew 28:19–20.

7. Think back. When has God used you to pursue another soul for his kingdom?

Day Three

Our Father pursues us through dreams.

Has God ever spoken to you through a dream? I have had two dreams about the second coming of Jesus Christ: one when I was sixteen and another more recently. In my second dream, I appeared to be much older and was possibly living in a stark nursing home (Not too exciting!). I heard the trumpet of God sound, I levitated off my bed, my clothes transformed into a lily-white robe, and then I penetrated the brick wall of the home and greeted Jesus in the air. It was a joyous moment, and it is because of these dreams I believe Jesus will return in my lifetime.

Revelatory dreams are happening frequently in the Middle East. Muslims may not be open to Jesus Christ as Savior, but they are open to an insightful dream. *Mission Frontiers Magazine* says out of 600 converts in the Middle East, one out of four have had a dream from God.[1] According to the Gospel Coalition, in these dreams:

- Jesus is speaking Scripture to them, even Scripture they had never heard before.
- Jesus tells people to do something.
- The dreams or visions lead to a feeling of being clean or at peace.
- A man in white physically appears.[2]

In today's study, we will examine a case in the Bible of the Holy Spirit speaking through a dream or vision to one of Jesus' disciples, Philip, and how the dream led Philip to reach out to a seeker of God.

1. Read Acts 8:26–40.

---

[1] Carlson, Darren. "When Muslims Dream of Jesus." The Gospel Coalition. https://www.thegospelcoalition.org/article/muslims-dream-jesus/ (accessed March 4, 2019).
[2] Ibid.

2. What was Philip doing when he received the word to go south to the road that goes down from Jerusalem to Gaza?

3. What was the eunuch reading and what was his question?

4. How did Philip respond?

5. What did the eunuch do once he believed?

6. What happened to Philip after that?

7. Has the Holy Spirit ever pursued you through a dream or vision? What was the result?

Day Four

Our Father pursues us through inspirational messages.

One of my friends, Cecilia, whose story is included in the chapter, "My Father's Restoration" of *The Only Father I Ever Knew,* had a physically and verbally abusive father, so she didn't have a positive father image growing up. One day, when Cecilia was a little girl, she was in a Sunday school class where the teacher told the class that Jesus loved them and would protect those he loved from harm. It was then that she began to falsely believe that Jesus didn't love her since she had not been protected from her abusive dad, so on that day she decided she wasn't going to love him either.

Years later, her husband announced he wanted to attend church, so she went along, solely to support him and without any belief that this would lead to a relationship with her heavenly Father. However, the pastor's sermon shocked her as he shared a story about abuse like the abuse she experienced. Afterward, he said, "If you were ever abused, I am truly sorry." Cecilia had never heard those apologetic words, but it was enough to explore a relationship with her heavenly Father. What Cecilia found, which is truth for all of us, is that we cannot equate a relationship with God to our earthly father relationships. He is far above that. Humans are flawed because they have free will and often make bad choices, but God is perfect. He wants the best for us and pursues us so we will discover all this for ourselves.

Today we will look at how God pursued thousands of people through the Beatitudes found in Jesus' Sermon on the Mount.

1. Read Matthew 5:1–12.

2. What did Jesus do when he saw the crowds?

3. What all does Jesus call "blessed"?

4. As you look at all that is considered blessed, in what area is Jesus pursuing you to improve?

5. Why should we rejoice and be glad?

6. How has God pursued you through an inspirational message?

7. Has your heavenly Father ever used you to deliver a message? If so how did it change a life?

Day Five

Our Father pursues us through circumstances.

Mary Ann doesn't remember much about her earthly father because he took his own life when she was three. She and her siblings grew up in difficult circumstances and were left out of cheerleader, band, and sports tryouts because they couldn't afford the uniforms. Mary Ann's Scottish-born mom got tired of being labeled the "suicide mom," so one day she packed up her family and moved from their small town to the big city. That's where Mary Ann's heavenly Father heard her cries of, "Papa, where are you? I need you. I need you to hold me and protect me."

God answered Mary Ann's prayer by opening up a door to play on her high school volleyball team, then by providing a scholarship to be part of a college volleyball team that ended up winning three straight national championships. When Mary Ann later looked back on these circumstances, she realized God was faithful and provided what she needed every step of the way.

Through the story of Joash, the Israelite king, let's see how God pursued this young boy during the worst of circumstances.

1. Read 2 Chronicles 22.

2. What did Athaliah, the mother of Ahaziah, want to do?

3. How did God save Joash?

4. Read 2 Chronicles 23.

5. What happened to Athaliah?

6. In 2 Chronicles 24:1–2, how old was Joash when he became king, and how did he rule?

7. When has God pursued you through difficult circumstances?

Week Two: Forgiver

I was participating in a study of the book of Romans when I finally understood the depth of God's forgiveness in my life. The Bible study began with an exercise based on Romans 1:21–25. The passage says, "For although they knew God, they neither glorified him as God nor gave thanks to him, but their thinking became futile and their foolish hearts were darkened. Although they claimed to be wise, they became fools and exchanged the glory of the immortal God for images made to look like a mortal human being and birds and animals and reptiles. Therefore God gave them over in the sinful desires of their hearts to sexual impurity for the degrading of their bodies with one another. They exchanged the truth about God for a lie, and worshiped and served created things rather than the Creator—who is forever praised. Amen."

The study then asked me to replace the word "they" with my name. It looked like this: "For although **Lisa** knew God, **Lisa** neither glorified him as God nor gave thanks to him, but **Lisa's** thinking became futile and **Lisa's** foolish heart was darkened. Although **Lisa** claimed to be wise, **Lisa** became fools and exchanged the glory of the immortal God for images made to look like a mortal human being and birds and animals and reptiles. Therefore God gave **Lisa** over in the sinful desires of **Lisa's** heart to sexual impurity for the degrading of **Lisa's** body with one another. **Lisa** exchanged the truth about God for a lie, and worshiped and served created things rather than the Creator—who is forever praised. Amen."

After I completed this exercise, the blinders came off my eyes about my sinful behavior in college, as well as in my twenties before I was married. I had traded my relationship with God for popularity and had fallen into a pattern of sexual promiscuity in my search for love. I finally realized that there is only one perfect love, and that flows from our heavenly Father. No other love satisfies. However, it was through this experience I discovered grace and God's forgiveness. In this week's study, we will look at the forgiveness of God through the eyes of the Word so we can better understand this attribute of God.

Day One

Our Father forgives us when we turn away from him.

Not all of us accept Jesus Christ as our Lord and Savior and stick with it throughout our lifetime. I personally had two encounters, salvation in high school and rededication in my early thirties after a devastating job loss in my television career. I had been disconnected from God for seventeen years, and there is no power in that. I was a prodigal child who came back to my heavenly Father, hopeless and lost, and he welcomed me with open arms. Today, based on the parable of the lost son found in Luke 15, we will see how God welcomes us when we return to him after an extended time of estrangement.

1. Read Luke 15:11–32.

2. What did the younger son decide to do and what was the end result?

3. After the younger son squandered his money, what realization came to him?

4. Where was the father standing and how did he react when his son returned?

5. How did the father respond to the jealous older son?

6. This is a parable about our heavenly Father's forgiveness. Who are you in this story?

7. Were you, or are you, a prodigal? If so, how does it feel to know that God is watching for your return with open arms?

Day Two

Our Father forgives us when we
deny him before others.

Are you timid about sharing your faith with others? Sometimes we are afraid that we'll be left out of events if we're perceived as a Bible thumper so we remain silent about spiritual things. Another way we can deny God is by not spending time with him each day, replacing a quiet time with our "to do" lists. Let's look at why it's important to remain faithful to our heavenly Father.

1. Read Matthew 26:31–35 and Luke 22:54–62.

2. In the first passage, what did Jesus predict about Peter?

3. In the Luke passage, how did Peter fulfill Jesus' prophecy about him?

4. What did Peter do after he realized he'd denied Jesus?

5. Read Isaiah 55:7. What must we do to stay connected to God?

6. Read Matthew 6:33. What do you think "all these things" means in your life?

7. Reflect on your life. Has there ever been a time when you've denied Jesus? If so, when? How did he forgive you?

Day Three

Our Father forgives us when we don't follow his instruction.

The Israelites were notorious for obeying God for a while, then forgetting what they've learned. It cost them an extra forty-year stay in the wilderness, but despite all the roaming around, God still offered forgiveness when his people humbled themselves and returned to his ways. Even though they were sinful, he still fed them manna from heaven and gave them water to drink. When most of the first refugees from Egypt died off, in God's abundant forgiveness, he allowed their children to enter the Promised Land. In the same way, if we have accepted Jesus as our Lord and Savior, we are sealed by the Holy Spirit and will enter the Promised Land of eternity with God, even though we, too, are disobedient at times. In this day's lesson, we will look at examples of how God received the Israelites back when they returned to him by repenting of their sins.

1. Read Zechariah 1:1–6

2. What does God want his people to do and what does he promise in return?

3. This word from God through the prophet Zechariah was given toward the end of the Israelites' Babylonian captivity, allowed because of their disobedience to God. How did the Israelites respond to God's plea through Zechariah?

4. Read Zechariah 8:14–17. What did God promise to do because of Israel's repentance?

5. What does God ask the Israelites to do in return for his forgiveness?

6. Read James 1:22–25. What does this passage say about those who don't follow the instruction of God's Word? What does it say about those who act on his Word?

7. Have you ever not followed God's instruction? What was the result?

Day Four

Our Father forgives us for all of our past and current sins.

Years ago, there was a popular movie called *Back to the Future.* In it, Marty McFly, a seventeen-year-old high school student was accidentally sent thirty years into the past in a time-traveling DeLorean invented by his close friend, scientist Doc Brown. In the movie, Marty met his high-school-aged parents, and knowing what he knew, his interaction with them couldn't help but make some dramatic changes in who his parents grew up to be.

Sometimes I wish I could go back as an adult and warn my younger self about not engaging in sinful behavior. I long to return to the past and prevent myself from making the mistakes I made in college. However, because God has forgiven me for how I behaved in my late teens and twenties, I have a good handle on what grace looks like. Are you thankful for God's forgiveness of past and current sins?

1. Read Psalm 103:10–12. Do we receive the punishment we deserve for our sins? How wide-reaching is God's forgiveness?

2. Read Romans 5:8–11. How has God reconciled us to him?

3. Ephesians 2:1–5. What did we deserve for our sin?

4. Have you ever prayed to receive Jesus Christ as your Lord and Savior? It's as simple as ABC.

- Admit you have fallen short of the glory of God and have committed sin.
- Believe that Jesus Christ is the Son of God; died on the cross to bear our past and future sins; and on the third day after his death, rose again and now sits at the right hand of God the Father.
- Commit your life to him from this day forward.

5. If you have already made this commitment, give a synopsis of the day you repented of your sin and gave your life to Jesus Christ.

6. How grateful are you for forgiveness of sins?

7. How have you shared this good news with others?

Day Five

Our Father forgives us for the wrongs
we commit against others.

I rededicated my life to Christ while living in Connecticut, but God's first order of business for my life was to return to my home town of San Antonio and to forgive my mother for harboring any resentment against her for the neglect in my life. By that time, my mother, who never recovered from my father's sudden death, was living in a group home. Forgiving her meant visiting her regularly, providing for her needs, and eventually learning to love her and have compassion for her. In today's study, reflect on God's forgiveness for you, and ask him to reveal who you need to forgive in return.

1. Read Matthew 18:21–35.

2. How many times did Jesus tell Peter we should forgive a brother or sister who sins against us?

3. How did the king respond to the servant's plea for mercy? How did the servant treat the fellow servant?

4. What happened to the original servant? In verse 35, how does this apply to us?

5. Read Matthew 5:23–24. What does this passage say about reconciliation?

6. Is there anyone you need to forgive as your Father has forgiven you?

Week Three: Teacher

But I don't want to stay home from school! Did you ever say that as a child? Maybe not, but I was one of those geeky kids who loved school and had to be forced to remain home when I was sick. Sometimes, even when I was under the weather, I would still attempt to go to my classes, only to be shown the exit later in the day.

I haven't changed, and my favorite place of discovery is the Bible. The Word of God is more than a history book like some believe. It is "alive and active. Sharper than any double-edged sword" (Hebrews 4:12) and teaches us how to live on a daily basis. The Bible contains everything we need to be a survivor in a topsy-turvy world. It is our lifeline—the spiritual food that sustains us. So this week, we will enter God's classroom and do a quick tour of some of the subjects found in our heavenly Father's curriculum.

Day One

Our Father teaches us his ways.

When Moses was called by God to lead his people out of captivity in Egypt, it's probably good that the great I Am didn't share all the details of Moses' future as he commissioned him from the burning bush. It might have been T.M.I., and God probably didn't want Moses to hide in the sheep pen. Because during the Israelites forty years of wandering in the wilderness, through Moses, God issued the Ten Commandments and 613 additional Levitical laws. He also taught Moses how to build a church, or in this case, a tabernacle, something that had not previously existed. In today's reading, we will see how God teaches specifically and leaves out no detail when he instructs us.

1. Read Exodus 25:1–9. What did God ask his people to make?

2. Did God leave the blueprint up to the Israelites' imagination?

3. Read Exodus 25:10–22. Describe the Ark of the Covenant. What was placed in it?

4. Read Exodus 25:23–40. What did the table and lampstand look like?

5. What specific instruction did God give in verse 40?

6. Skim through Exodus 26. Name some of the tabernacle details that stand out to you.

7. Read 1 Thessalonians 5:24. Has God ever provided you with detailed instructions for a project that you felt called to? Share about the experience.

Day Two

Our Father uses his Word to teach us.

After I prayed to receive Jesus Christ in high school, I was a follower for a while. I attended church with my friend and was exposed to the things of God but fell away when I went off to college. Unfortunately, the pursuit of popularity and boys choked out my pursuit of God. I was estranged from my heavenly Father for another seventeen years. However, after my traumatic job loss, I spiraled and needed stability. Because of that I returned to the foundation I had learned in high school. I joined a church and attended a Bible study, reading the Word of God regularly for the first time in my life. It was through this discipline of reading the Bible and prayer that I began to see changes in my life and felt God's presence in a way I'd never experienced before. Today, as we look at how our heavenly Father teaches us through his Word, we will discover the importance of staying connected to the Bible and how that divine connection can change your life.

1. Read Hebrews 4:12. What does this verse mean when it says the Word of God is "alive and active" and "sharper than any double-edged sword"?

2. Read 2 Timothy 3:16–17. How is Scripture useful? How does it equip us?

3. Read Psalm 119:105, Luke 11:28, Matthew 4:4, Matthew 7:24, and John 15:7. What benefit do we receive from reading the Word of God?

4. Read John 1:1–4 and John 1:14. Who is the Word?

5. How does this understanding of the Word bring the Word to life?

6. How has God pursued you through his Word?

7. Why is it important to stay connected to the Word of God?

Day Three

**Our Father teaches us what's true and negates
the lies of the enemy.**

What are some of the lies you speak to yourself? Here are mine: *You're not pretty enough. You're not loved. You're a has-been.* However, the Word of God assures us that we are created in God's image, so we are beautiful in his eyes. God promises that he loves us with an unfailing love, and even though some of us have not achieved the same success in a second career as the first, we have to believe that God has us right where he wants us. When the devil tempted Jesus in the desert, Jesus came up with the antidote to Satan's lies—truths from Scripture, and through the Word, counteracted all of the enemy's claims. In today's study, let's fill our minds with God's truth rather than the lies of the enemy.

1. Read Psalm 25:5. What was David asking of God in this verse that is available to all of us today?

2. Read Matthew 4:3, Revelation 12:10, and John 8:44. How is Satan described?

3. Read Romans 8:1, 1 Peter 5:9, and Ephesians 6:13–18. What are some ways to overcome the lies of the devil?

4. Read 2 Corinthians 10:5. According to this verse, when lies begin to seep through our minds, what are we to do?

5. Read John 14:6, John 1:1–5, and John 1:14. Who does the Bible say Jesus is?

6. If Jesus is the Word that became flesh, how important is it to believe what the Word says about you?

7. What lies have you believed about yourself? After today's truths, how will you overcome them?

Day Four

Our Father teaches us what to say
in difficult situations.

A friend called me recently and wanted advice about a dilemma she was in concerning a board where she served. After staging a successful fundraiser, she was surprisingly asked to resign from the board the following day. She was perplexed about how to handle the situation and didn't know how to proceed. I didn't have clarity on how to advise her so I prayed silently in the middle of our conversation, asking *What should I say?* I felt like the Lord told me to give it over to him in prayer, because he is the defender of our battles, so we prayed together. Following our prayer, my friend went to a new hair salon and saw a woman she recognized. As it turned out, it was a board member from the same board that wanted to release her. The board member had never been to that salon before. Coincidence? When my friend shared what was going on concerning her dismissal, this board member promised to support her and try to get the decision overturned. God showed me what to say in a difficult situation, and the result was supernatural. Today, we'll study the biblical story of another great man of faith, Nehemiah, to see how he handled a ticklish scenario.

1. Read Nehemiah 1:1–11. What was Nehemiah upset about?

2. Read Nehemiah 2:1–6. What was the king of Persia's (Artaxerxes) question for Nehemiah?

3. What did Nehemiah do before he responded?

4. What was Nehemiah's request?

5. How did the king respond?

6. Do you think Nehemiah's prayer impacted the king's favorable decision? If so, why?

7. Has God ever provided the words for you when there were no words? If not, how will you implement this practice in your own life?

Day Five

Our Father teaches us new things.

When I start my morning quiet time, I often say, "Lord, show me something in your Word that I've never seen before." He is always faithful. Jeremiah 33:3 says, "Call to me and I will answer you and tell you great and unsearchable things you do not know." Our heavenly Father wants to stretch us and expand our horizon. He'd like for us to see our lives and other people from his perspective and desires to teach us revelatory things through his Word.

I am a blogger, so during Christmastime, I asked God to show me something new about the Christmas story. I was skeptical because I thought I knew the Christmas story backward and forward, but the Lord revealed something I'd never seen before. Maybe it will be new for you as well, as we use this as an example of how our Father loves to teach us new things.

1. Read Luke 2:8–20.

2. What did the angel of the Lord announce to the shepherds?

3. What did the shepherds decide to do after the heavenly host appeared with the angel?

4. What did they do after they saw Mary, Joseph, and baby Jesus?

5. In verse 20, what does it say the shepherds did after spreading the word about Jesus?

6. Did you know that the shepherds made two visits to see Jesus? Was that new for you? In the busyness of the Christmas season, what if, when all the presents are unwrapped and the dinner is over, we returned like the shepherds and worshipped Jesus?

7. Has God ever shown you something new in his Word? Write down a couple of examples. If not, begin to pray daily that he will give you new insight into who he is.

"See, I am doing a new thing! Now it springs up; do you not perceive it?" — Isaiah 43:19

Week Four: Healer

I attended a retreat recently and was speaking to a woman about our college years. She had been a chemistry and biology double major. I was a communications major. I said, "Biology was always my worst subject in both high school and college. Kind of surprising since my father was a medical doctor." It was at that moment I heard the Holy Spirit say: "You may not be a doctor, but I gifted you to heal." I was taken aback, but it was a confirmation of the gifting I received. My ministry, Pearls of Promise, is an emotional healing ministry. My heart is for people to heal both emotionally and physically, and God, as Jehovah Rapha, uses me and many others as his conduit to heal. In this week's lesson, we will reveal our heavenly Father's heart to heal us—emotionally, physically, and spiritually.

Day One

Our Father heals disease.

God can use anyone as a vessel for healing, and I am one of those he occasionally calls on to lay hands on the sick. I have seen the Lord remove cancer, lower blood pressure, heal a damaged vocal cord, repair an ailing foot, smooth out inflamed skin, disintegrate a troublesome nodule, and turn back the effects of diabetes. Our Father in Heaven still heals today. However, to activate supernatural healing, we must believe God is a healer. Today, we will study how God heals infirmities.

1. Read Matthew 8:5–13. What was going on with the centurion's servant?

2. When Jesus asked the centurion if he wanted him to go and heal his servant, how did the centurion respond?

3. Was the servant healed?

4. Do you believe we can call upon the name of Jesus to heal today? If so, explain your answer.

5. Read Psalm 103:3 and Jeremiah 17:14. What do these verses say?

6. How many diseases does Psalm 103 say God heals? Then why is it important that we believe he still heals today?

7. What kind of healing do you need? Ask God for healing, believing he still heals. James 4:2 says, "You do not have because you do not ask God." If you are in a small group, take a moment to pray God's healing over each other.

Day Two

Our Father heals our broken hearts.

Has human love ever let you down? While I am happily married, I still remember an earlier relationship where my heart was shattered by a boyfriend. It took time and a lot of Kleenex to pick up the pieces and move on. But God promises in Psalm 147:3 that he "heals the brokenhearted and binds up their wounds." So today, let's see the Father's heart to heal our emotional wounds.

1. Read John 4:4–42. In verse 10, what water did Jesus want to give the Samaritan woman?

2. Read John 7:7–39. What is the living water?

3. Through belief in Jesus Christ, we receive the Holy Spirit, and it is the Spirit of God that helps us attain emotional healing. What did the Samaritan woman need healing from (John 4:16–18)?

4. How did the Samaritan woman respond to her encounter with Jesus (John 4:28–29)?

5. How did this woman's emotional healing impact others (John 4:39)?

6. For those who were still skeptical, how did Jesus reach them (John 4:40–42)?

7. Read Psalm 34:18 and Isaiah 53:5. Have you ever given your emotional wounds over to Jesus? If so, how did he heal you?

Day Three

Our Father heals our sinfulness.

As hard as we try to be righteous, there is still a sinful nature lurking around the corner. Whether it's anger, judgmental thoughts, or coveting, sinfulness is something we've all inherited, and there's only one answer for healing of the human condition: total surrender of our lives to Jesus Christ. First Peter 2:24 says, "'He himself bore our sins' in his body on the cross, so that we might die to sins and live for righteousness; 'by his wounds you have been healed.'" There is no sin, no shortcoming, and no crime that the Son of God can't heal because of his sacrifice. Today, we will examine God's healing of the wrongdoing in our lives.

1. Read Luke 7:36–50. What did the sinful woman do with the alabaster flask of oil?

2. Why do you think this act represented repentance from the woman's heart?

3. According to the short parable Jesus told in verses 40 to 42, how much of our sin or "debt" does God forgive when we are repentant?

4. Did Jesus forgive the woman's sin (verse 48)?

5. How has Jesus forgiven you?

6. While we can't physically see Jesus today, what are ways you can thank him?

7. Read Psalm 51:10 and Philippians 4:13. It is easy to fall back into sin if we are not careful. What are some things we can do to avoid going backwards in our Christian walk?

Day Four

Our Father heals our minds.

When I moved from South Texas to North Texas, I never dreamed the transition would be so difficult. I was no longer working in a public profession like television or public relations. I was now attending seminary and taking care of my two boys. I had no close friends, I began to worry about my husband at his workplace, and I drifted into a situational depression. However, God healed my thinking through a variety of ways, and today, I possess supernatural strength that can only derive from my heavenly Father. In today's lesson, we'll see how the Lord can turn our stinkin' thinkin' around.

1. Read about the story of Jehoshaphat in 2 Chronicles 20: 14–30
   This passage is about fighting the enemies of the Israelites, the
   Ammonites, the Moabites, and the people of Mount Seir. What
   did the Spirit of God say through Jahaziel about the battle
   (verse 17)?

2. Instead of fighting the traditional way, what did the Israelites do
   (verse 21)?

3. What action did the Lord take while his people were singing
   praises to him (verses 22–24)?

4. How can we defeat the enemies of our soul (negative thoughts and the lies we tell ourselves) by praising God in the midst of it?

5. Read Psalm 100:4. How do we enter God's presence? Do you think that our unhealthy thoughts can survive in the presence of God?

6. Read 2 Corinthians 10:5 and Philippians 4:8. When we know our thinking is not godly or does not line up with the promises of Scripture, what should we do?

7. Read Romans 12:2. In what way does your mind need renewing and healing?

Day Five

Our Father uses us to heal others.

I remember the first time God used me as a conduit for healing. I was working as the public relations manager at an airport when EMS was called to help one of my employees whose blood pressure spiked. When I saw her, I immediately felt compassion, laid a hand on her head, and prayed silently. She later told me she felt like that was the moment her blood pressure began to lower and said she knew what I was doing. However, for a while, this call to heal was used sporadically. I stored the gift away in the attic, because I still didn't believe God could use me in this way, and quite frankly, the gift scared me. However, as I've matured spiritually, I've come to the realization that I need to walk in faith and utilize the gift of healing. God has called me to pray over many friends who have struggled physically, and I've witnessed numerous miraculous healings. However, I am not the only one God uses in this way. He can use you as his vessel as well to facilitate healing. Today, we will look at how he used ordinary people to do extraordinary acts of healing.

1. Read Matthew 10:5–8. When Jesus sent the twelve disciples out without him, what did he tell them to do?

2. Read Acts 5:12–16. This took place after Jesus' ascension. Describe what the apostles were doing?

3. Read John 14:12–14. Jesus' primary ministry was healing. What does this passage say that believers will be able to accomplish?

4. Read Matthew 17:14–20. How did Jesus heal in this passage?

5. Why didn't the disciples have success?

6. Why is belief an important prerequisite for healing?

7. Has God ever used you as a conduit for his healing? Has the Lord ever used anyone else to heal you? Explain.

Week Five: Builder

My grandfather was an architect who designed thousands of homes in South Texas, many of which are still standing. However, to save his client's money, he also took on the contractor role and watched over the building process. That meant his job was not finished once the blueprints were created. He traveled to job sites and brick-by-brick, watched the homes he created take shape and come to life. That must have been thrilling for him. In the same way, I believe God is like an architect/builder who is thrilled to see his creation, you, take shape. He has a supernatural interest in you and doesn't want to see his building crumble. This week, we'll look at how our heavenly Father builds us.

Day One

Our Father builds our bodies.

I haven't always been happy with the way I look. What about you? However, as I've grown to understand more about God's creation, I realize when we complain about our physical appearance, or our internal makeup, we are criticizing God's design. He built us just the way he wanted us, and we are intricately put together. In my chapter "My Father's Creation" found in *The Only Father I Ever Knew,* I provided some interesting facts about the human body:

- Messages from the human brain travel along nerves at up to 200 miles per hour.
- A human's little finger contributes over 50 percent of the hand's strength.
- A human skeleton renews itself completely every ten years.
- The brain contains eighty-six billion nerve cells joined by one hundred trillion connections. This is more than the number of stars in the Milky Way.
- Every hour, humans shed about 600,000 particles of skin—about 1.4 pounds every year.
- In an adult human, blood circulates about 12,000 miles a day. That is like traveling from east to west across the widest part of the Pacific Ocean.[3]

This week we will discover how our heavenly Father built us and how he continues to build us throughout our lives.

1. Read Psalm 139:13. When did God first start building us?

---

[3] Karen Lehnardt, "56 Amazing Facts About the Human Body," FactRetriever, https://www.factretriever.com/body-facts (accessed October 23, 2017).

2. Read Genesis 1:26–27. In whose image are we created?

3. Knowing you are created in the image of God, how does that change the way you think about your looks?

4. Read Ezekiel 36:26–27. When we accept Jesus as our Lord and Savior, how does God rebuild our hearts?

5. In Ephesians 3: 16–17, who resides in your building?

6. How does that impact the way you look at your body?

7. How has today's study spoken to you?

Day Two

Our Father builds a firm foundation.

God has already poured the slab for our lives, Jesus Christ. The Bible says Jesus has been laid as a firm foundation for all of us, whether we acknowledge it or not. How we build on this foundation is up to us. Will we construct our house with quality materials or will we compromise the building process with cheap building supplies? Will we allow the Maker full access to be the contractor over our spiritual house?

1. Read Psalm 127:1. What happens when we try to build our lives without God?

2. Read 1 Corinthians 3:9–17. Whose building are we?

3. Who is the foundation?

4. What are some examples of solid building materials in a Christian's life?

5. What happens to work that is not of God? What will the believer receive if his/her work endures the fire?

6. Who resides in your building (1 Corinthians 3:16)? How does having a holy God as a tenant affect how you live?

7. How have you built your house so far? Does your building need some remodeling?

Day Three

Our Father builds our faith.

We all meander in our faith at one time or another. When I begin to question, I look at the intricacy of my body and creation, and I think of the times that God spoke directly to me. In the Old Testament, when one of the patriarchs had a close encounter with God, they'd build an altar or name the spot of the divine meeting to recognize the Lord's presence with them and to let others witness where the Almighty had appeared.

Jacob had a story like this. After Jacob wrestled with the Angel of the Lord all night to receive a blessing, he called the place Peniel, saying, "It is because I saw God face to face, and yet my life was spared."

These markers are a place to rewind back to when we struggle and our faith begins to dip. While the Lord seems distant during the winter seasons of our lives, we make it through the cold spells by recalling a different time when the warmth of the Lord was so close we could almost touch him. Do you recall a time, or a stretch of time, when you felt God's intervention in your life? You need to mark it in your mind. In today's study, we'll see that even the early disciples struggled with faith.

1. Read Mark 9:14–29. What was wrong with the boy?

2. When Jesus asked the boy's father, "How long has he been like this?" what did the boy's father say (verse 22)?

3. How did Jesus respond to the father in verse 23?

4. What did the father exclaim in verse 24?

5. Through the teaching of this passage, what should we do when our own faith waffles?

6. Read Hebrews 11:1 and James 1:6. What is the definition of faith? Why is it important not to doubt God?

7. How does your faith need building? Pray for your Father to increase your faith.

Day Four

Our Father builds our character.

As a fatherless child with an emotionally unstable mother, I did not receive direction on how to carry myself, how to act around people, or the difference between right and wrong. Early on, I made a lot of mistakes and said a lot of things I wish I could take back, but after I rededicated my life to Christ and became a follower of Jesus, the Lord began to shape my character to be more like his. My career was no longer my main focus. Instead, I desired to please God and wanted to be in the center of his will. Today, we will look at how God transforms us from the inside out to be a building of light that glorifies him.

1. Read 2 Corinthians 5:17. What do we become when we believe in Jesus Christ?

2. Acts 9:1–22. How did Jesus reveal himself to Saul (Paul)?

3. In verse 18, what did Saul do once he regained his vision?

4. According to verse 20, how fast did Saul preach about Jesus?

5. Read Galatians 1:13–24 and Philippians 3:12. In these passages, how did Paul's passion change?

6. Read Galatians 5:22–23 and Colossians 3:12–15. How can God change our character through the power of the Holy Spirit?

7. What fruits of the spirit do you excel in? What do you still desire? As you look at Colossians 3:12–15, what are some of the areas of your character where you desire to improve?

Day Five

Our Father desires for us to build up others.

With the encouragement we receive from God throughout our building process, God wants us to pay it forward and encourage others, so that they are built up. We are also called to comfort others in the midst of trials. Have you ever walked through something difficult, felt like God brought you through it, and then he placed someone in front of you with the exact issue that you overcame? It was not a coincidence. God desires for us to build up others. This week, let's look at the various ways we can encourage and build up our sisters and brothers.

1. Read 1 Thessalonians 5:1–15. This passage speaks about end times. If time is short before Jesus returns, what should we be doing (verse 11)?

2. According to verses 12 and 13, how should we treat those who are at work around us?

3. In verses 14 through 16, what else are we supposed to do?

4. Read 2 Corinthians 1:3–4. After God comforts us in our troubles, how should we respond?

5. Read Proverbs 11:25. What happens when we take the time to encourage someone else?

6. According to Proverbs 16:24, what is another benefit of building someone else up through encouragement?

7. When is the last time you encouraged someone? What was the result? Who do you need to build up today?

Week Six: Lover

Think about the time that you were most in love, then multiply that love by infinity. The love we experience on this earth is just a shadow of the love that our Abba Father has for us. He is the one who created the feeling of love that we experience. In fact, Scripture says that God *is* love (1 John 4:7). God created love because he desires for us to enter into an *agape* (the highest expression of love—pure, selfless, and unconditional) relationship with all of us. Out of love, he created us. Because of his love, we have a mind and free will to choose him as Father, and thanks to his love, we are given an opportunity to spend eternity in his presence. In the final week of this study on *Knowing the Father*, we dive head first into the endless sea of God's love and will discover the attributes of his love for us.

Day One

Our Father's love is eternal.

If you didn't marry your high school or college sweetheart, you've probably deduced that love doesn't always last. Perhaps you had a parent who fell short in the love category. The good news is that there is a love that never fails us and never fades: God's love. First Chronicles 16:34 says, "Give thanks to the Lord, for he is good; his love endures forever." Sometimes the enemy of your soul will attempt to make you believe God doesn't care about you. Rebuke that thought and trust what God says about his love in his Word. Today, let's bask in the infinite love of God.

1. Read Psalm 89:2, Psalm 107:1, and Psalm 136: 1. What's the life span of God's love?

2. Read 1 Corinthians 13:1–13 to find out the characteristics of God's love.

3. What are we if we don't have love (verse 1)?

4. How does this passage describe those who do not have love (verses 2–3)?

5. What will happen to prophecies and tongues? In turn, what will happen to love (verses 8–9)?

6. Can you think of an example of how God has shown his love to you?

7. What are some ways you can love as God loves? Are you feeling more loved as you look at God's never-ending love?

Day Two

Our Father's love is overflowing.

This year, the Holy Spirit gave me new insight into Ephesians 3:17–19 that says, "And I pray that you, being rooted and established in love, may have power, together with all the Lord's holy people to grasp now wide and long and high and deep is the love of Christ, and to know this love that surpasses knowledge—that you may be filled to the measure of all the fullness of God." We need God's power to understand how much he loves us! I realized that we humans simply don't have the mental capacity to understand the vastness of God's love. That's why we occasionally struggle with feeling unloved by the heavenly Father. Today, let's tap into God's overflowing love for us and attempt to wrap our thoughts around the depth of that love for us.

1. Read Ephesians 3:16–19. What does this passage say we need in order to understand the depth of God's love for us?

2. What does this love surpass (verse 19)?

3. What does God want to do with his love (verse 19)?

4. Read Psalm 119:64. What does God's love fill?

5. Read Psalm 36:5. How high does God's love reach?

6. Read Psalm 86:5. Describe God's love when we call upon him.

7. Have you experienced the greatness of God's love in your life? Based on what you learned today, what do you need to do to get a handle on the overflowing love of God for you?

Day Three

Our Father wants us to be vessels of his love.

We are God's ambassadors on this earth, and if we are to represent him well, we need to be filled to the brim with his love. God wants us to love our enemies and love those around us who need a little extra patience. He calls us to love our spouse and to love the Christian brothers and sisters he places in our lives. Let's examine how we can be better lovers of God's people.

1. Read 1 John 4:7–8. What does this passage say about those who do not love?

2. Read Matthew 5:43–48. Who does God want us to love?

3. Why should we not love only those who love us?

4. Read John 13:34–35. God commands us to love others. What will people realize about us if we honor this commandment?

5. Read 1 Thessalonians 3:12. If we are lacking in love for others, who can increase our capacity to love?

6. Read 1 Peter 4:8. What does it mean by "love covers a multitude of sins"?

7. Who needs God's love in your world? How can you better love the difficult people in your life?

Day Four

Our Father desires our love in return.

God created love, so we'd choose to love him back. I know I don't love God the way he'd like for me to love him, and I often pray, *Help me to love you more, Lord.* As a reminder to pour out love to God, I've posted the words of what Jesus described as the "greatest commandment" over the door to my garage: "Love the Lord your God with all your heart, and with all your soul, and with all your strength." Every time I leave the house, I'm reminded that loving God and his children is the most important thing I could possibly do that day. Today, let's see what the Bible says about loving our heavenly Father.

1. Read Deuteronomy 6:4–9. How are we to love God?

2. What are we supposed to do with this commandment?

3. Read Matthew 22:36–40. Jesus was asked by a Pharisee to name the greatest commandment. What did he say? What was the second greatest? What did he say hangs on these two commandments?

4. Read John 14:23–24 and 1 John 5:3. What is one important way we can show our love to God?

5. Read John 15:12–14. What is another way we can demonstrate love for our heavenly Father?

6. Read Proverbs 8:17 and 1 Corinthians 2:9. When we love God, what does the Word say that God gives us in return?

7. On a scale of 1 to 10, with 10 being the best, where does your love of God rank? What are some practical ways you can love God more?

Day Five

Our Father's love is sacrificial.

I may never be able to comprehend what God did for us when he sacrificed his own Son, Jesus, so that we might live with him forever. It's the greatest act of love ever recorded. We often see this verse displayed by a zealous fan at a sporting event: "For God so loved the world that he gave his only begotten Son, that whosoever believes in him will not perish but have everlasting life" (John 3:16). Could you imagine sacrificing your own child so that another might live? It's a love beyond comprehension, and because of this love, we can call God, Father. For a fatherless girl like me, there is no greater gift than God's reconciling love. In our final day, let's better understand the sacrificial love of God the Father.

1. Read Romans 5:8 and John 3:16. Why did God sacrifice his only Son?

2. Read 2 Corinthians 5:17–21. What did Christ's death on the cross and resurrection do for us?

3. As stated in Ephesians 1:7, what else do we receive?

4. According to Romans 8:1–4, what do we escape because of the sacrifice of Jesus on the cross?

5. Read 1 Peter 1:3–5. Because we are reconciled with God, what does our Father have waiting for us?

6. No matter what sins we have committed in the past, what does Jesus' sacrifice on the cross do to those sins that may have made us feel dirty (Isaiah 1:18)?

7. Can you put into words what God's sacrifice, out of love for you, means to you?

Epilogue

It is my hope that you have enjoyed this study, but more importantly that you have increased your scope of God as Father. In my own life, I've had to cast away any wrong thinking about Abba Daddy, and now base my image of God on what I read in Scripture about him. Through the Word, we discover God is loving, and he pursues us so we might choose a relationship with him. Once we accept his Son, Jesus, who sacrificed his life so we might be reconciled with God, we enter a journey, hand-in-hand with God the Father. He forgives us for all the wrong we committed. He teaches us his ways, builds our strength, heals our wounds, and demonstrates to us what it looks like to love as he loves.

He is the Dad of all dads and desires for us to be his children. He fills the void when our earthly dads were not around and is the perfect father we always longed for. Call upon him daily. Get to know him better by reading his Word. Tell him how much you love him. He desires to have a more intimate relationship with you, starting today.

Made in the USA
Lexington, KY
17 September 2019